Did Yo

PORTSM

A MISCELLANY

Compiled by Julia Skinner
With particular reference to the work of Sarah Quail

THE FRANCIS FRITH COLLECTION

www.francisfrith.com

Based on a book first published in the United Kingdom in 2005 by The Francis Frith Collection®

This edition published exclusively for Identity Books in 2012 ISBN 978-1-84589-392-7

British Library Cataloguing in Publication Data

Did You Know? Portsmouth - A Miscellany
Compiled by Julia Skinner
With particular reference to the work of Sarah Quail

The Francis Frith Collection
Oakley Business Park,
Wylye Road, Dinton,
Wiltshire SP3 5EU
Tel: +44 (0) 1722 716 376
Email: info@francisfrith.co.uk
www.francisfrith.com

Printed and bound in Malaysia
Contains material sourced from responsibly managed forests

Front Cover: **PORTSMOUTH, THE HARBOUR 1892** 30004p

The colour-tinting is for illustrative purposes only, and is not intended to be historically accurate

CONTENTS

PORTSMOUTH, HMS 'DUKE OF WELLINGTON'
1890 22755

INTRODUCTION

A key seafaring city and naval port since early times, Portsmouth evolved over the years into southern England's largest and most important naval base. Richard I was responsible for establishing a settlement on Portsea Island, and it was he who built the first dock here in the late 12th century.

Following Richard I's influence on Portsmouth, the Tudor kings, Henry VII and Henry VIII, constructed the first dry dock in the world here. Later the city played a key role in the defence of the British Empire, and became synonymous with the navy and Nelson's victory at Trafalgar, a link that is still kept vividly in the public imagination by the presence of Nelson's flagship HMS 'Victory' in Portsmouth's Historic Dockyard, where she keeps company with the Tudor warship the 'Mary Rose' and the iron-clad Victorian battleship HMS 'Warrior'.

The glory days of the empire may have gone now, but Portsmouth still retains its vital link with the sea, evoking not only images of England's fleets which have sailed from here to victory and defeat, but also of the many emigrants, naval officers and transported convicts on their way to Australia for whom the Sally Port represented one of their last views of England before they set off to some distant corner of the world.

**PORTSMOUTH, PUBLIC ART,
WYMERING COMMUNITY
CENTRE 2005** P100707k

PORTSMOUTH
WORDS AND PHRASES

'Scabs' - a local name for winkles.

'Squinny' - complain. Used either as a verb, as in 'don't squinny' (don't complain) or an adjective, as in 'she's really squinny' (she complains a lot).

'Lairy' or **'lair'** - cheeky, rude or aggressive.

'Dinlo' - an idiot, or dim-wit.

'Skait' or **'skate'** - a sailor.

'Genny' - generally.

'Scran' - a cold lunch taken to work.

'Treader' - bicycle.

'Puggled' - knocked silly.

'Weeee!' - a response to something startling, surprising or amazing.

'Hampshire Hog' - a person born in Hampshire.

'The Mucky Duck' - the White Swan pub.

'Turk Town' - Gosport.

'The hill' - Portsdown Hill. (North of the hill is 'The back of the hill'.)

Portsmouth's nickname is **'Pompey'**. It is not the prerogative of the football club to call itself by this name - the town, too, is known the world over as Pompey, but no one is exactly sure why. The most plausible reason relates to the story of the Portsmouth-based sailors who scaled Pompey's pillar in Alexandria in 1781 and toasted their success from the top with punch. Their efforts earned them the nickname 'the Pompey Boys'.

**PORTSMOUTH,
THE OLD MUNICIPAL
COLLEGE
2005** P100711k

HAUNTED PORTSMOUTH

Many theatres are said to be haunted, and Portsmouth's Theatre Royal is no exception. The ghost of an actor who killed himself by slitting his own throat in his dressing room of the Theatre Royal in the 1880s is said to haunt the building, particularly at the back of the auditorium.

One of Portsmouth's most famous haunted buildings is Wymering Manor, one of the oldest houses in the city. The building was investigated by television's 'Most Haunted Live' programme in 2006, when cold spots, strange tapping noises, and the sound of a baby crying were amongst the phenomena reported by the team.

The building now known as Buckingham House in the High Street was the scene in 1628 of the assassination of the Duke of Buckingham by James Felton, a discontented naval officer. Felton was subsequently hanged and gibbeted on Southsea Common, and ever since these tragic events the building has been believed to be haunted. Amongst the unexplained phenomena which have been reported at the location are strange noises including terrifying groans, light orbs and sudden changes in temperature.

The ghost of a barmaid who was murdered by her sailor husband when he returned home from sea is said to haunt the White Swan Inn in Guildhall Walk. Most of the reported paranormal activity has occurred in the cellar, where she met her death.

King's Bastion in Old Portsmouth is said to be haunted by 'Grey Ladies' and the shades of bewhiskered sailors.

Beware of standing on Blockhouse Point at the entrance to Portsmouth Harbour on dark and stormy nights, for it is said that you will hear the ghostly clanking of Jack the Painter's gibbet chains carried on the wind! The arsonist James Aitken, or 'Jack the Painter' as he was popularly known, was an anti-monarchist and an ardent supporter of the ideals of the American revolutionaries. He tried to burn down the dockyard in Portsmouth in 1776 but only the recently reconstructed ropehouse was destroyed. After fleeing to Bristol Jack was finally caught, tried and brought back to Portsmouth for execution. He was hanged from a ship's mizzen mast outside the main dockyard gate, and afterwards his body was gibbeted on Blockhouse Point.

**PORTSMOUTH, THE SPINNAKER
TOWER 2005** P100714k

SOUTHSEA, THE BEACH AND PIER 1898 42693

PORTSMOUTH, GUILDHALL SQUARE c1960 P100011

PORTSMOUTH MISCELLANY

The original Portsmouth was probably at the top of Portsmouth harbour, at the entrance to Fareham Creek.

The first English naval battle may well have taken place at the top of Portsmouth harbour in AD 896, between King Alfred's ships and six Viking boats.

The remains of a small Saxon boat were discovered in the mud at the top of Langstone Harbour in 2003.

The early history of Portsmouth is recorded in the Southwick Cartularies, the collection of documents relating to gifts made to Southwick Priory from its foundation.

Portsmouth's founder, Jean de Gisors, features in Dan Brown's blockbuster novel 'The Da Vinci Code' - as a member of the Order of Sion. There is no foundation to this particular part of the story.

Southwick Priory was established originally within the confines of Portchester Castle by Henry I in the 1120s. The canons moved over the hill to the village of Southwick in the mid 12th century.

Portsmouth's parish church is dedicated to St Thomas of Canterbury, not St Thomas the Apostle.

Richard I built a house for himself in Portsmouth. It was known as the King's House and occupied a site at the top of Penny Street, now part of Portsmouth Grammar School. The area was known as Kingshall Green until at least the 19th century.

There are references to a borough council, the predecessor of today's city council, as early as the 1230s.

According to the earliest local by-laws, the 'Customs and Usages', thieves had their ears nailed to the pillory in early medieval Portsmouth and scolds were immersed in the Camber on the ducking stool.

**PORTSMOUTH, THE BRITTANY FERRIES' SHIP
'MONT ST MICHEL' 2005** P100709k

PORTSMOUTH, THE ISLE OF WIGHT FERRY c1962 PI00035

**PORTSMOUTH, THE EMIGRANTS'
STATUE 2005** P100720k

PORTSMOUTH, ARTIST'S CORNER, THE SALLY PORT c1965 P100065

Portsmouth was raided by the French on at least four occasions during the Hundred Years' War.

The Garrison Church was a medieval hospice known as the Domus Dei, or God's House. From before the Reformation, it provided accommodation for pilgrims and strangers and cared for local people who needed nursing.

The first defences went up round Portsmouth in the late 14th century - an earthwork round the town itself and a tower, the precursor of the Round Tower, at the harbour entrance.

The people of Portsmouth were excommunicated in 1450 for the murder of the Bishop of Chichester within the precincts of the Domus Dei. It was said at the time that he was set upon by soldiers and sailors, aggrieved that they had not been paid their wages, but it was more likely a political assassination, procured by enemies of the king, Henry VI. Whatever the truth of the matter the church held Portsmouth and all its people responsible.

After the people of Portsmouth were excommunicated following the murder of the Bishop of Chichester in the town, they were not admitted back into the church until 1508, and only then after a most elaborate ceremony, during which the mayor and other leading townsfolk had to make their way on their knees from the Domus Dei, where the bishop was murdered, to the parish church, wearing penitential clothes.

Richard I built the first bridge over Portscreek. Henry VIII had the first bulwark constructed there to defend the crossing.

PORTSMOUTH, THE HARBOUR 1898 42705

PORTSMOUTH, THE HARD 1890 22751

The remains of a member of the ship's crew of the 'Mary Rose' were interred in the Cathedral on 19 July 1984.

The house where the Duke of Buckingham was assassinated in 1628 still stands at the top of the High Street. It is called 'Buckingham House'.

A fine monument to the Duke of Buckingham, erected by his sister, stands in St Thomas's Church.

Drunken troops, mainly Irish, fired live ammunition at worshippers in the parish church, killing some and severely wounding others, during the chaotic weeks of October 1688, before King James II fled the country and the Glorious Revolution put William and Mary on the throne.

By the end of the 17th century, Portsmouth was the most strongly defended town in the country and was the leading naval dockyard.

Thomas Wren, the minister of the High Street Presbyterian Chapel, was an advocate of the American cause during the War of Independence (1775-1782). He gave sanctuary to American seamen who had managed to escape from local prisons and arranged their passage, often in disguise, to London and further, usually to France.

PORTSMOUTH, THE HARBOUR 1892 30004

The lively overture 'Portsmouth Point' was composed by Sir William Walton in 1925. It was inspired by Thomas Rowlandson's cartoon of the same name of 1800 which depicts the lively atmosphere of Portsmouth and Pitsea at that date, when ships were preparing to go to sea or when they had returned from long voyages and victorious campaigns. Some of the characters that can be seen in the cartoon against a background of shipping and taverns are a drunken, peg-legged fiddler tripping over a mongrel dog, dockworkers going about their business, an old couple quarrelling vigorously in the foreground, and sailors cavorting with ladies of easy morals.

Marc Brunel's steam-driven block-making machinery, introduced into Portsmouth Dockyard in 1801, was the first example in the world of the use of metal machines for mass-production.

There is a remarkable collection of material relating to Portsmouth in the Turner Bequest in Tate Britain. J M W Turner visited the town at least four times and on each occasion he kept a sketchbook. Even today, the little line drawings are of clearly recognisable local scenes and places. Southsea Castle, the defences at the harbour entrance, St Thomas's, the dockyard and Gunwharf are particularly featured.

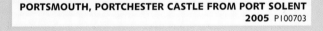

PORTSMOUTH, PORTCHESTER CASTLE FROM PORT SOLENT
2005 P100703

Portsmouth dockyard trebled in size from 99 to 261 acres between the middle and the end of the 19th century. The mid 19th century Great Extension was the last great territorial expansion of the dockyard and, like all previous expansions in earlier centuries, was once again driven by fears of French military ambitions.

PORTSMOUTH, THE HARBOUR, HMS 'ST VINCENT' 1890 22758

**PORTSMOUTH UNIVERSITY
LABORATORIES 2005**
P100712k

Portsmouth Theatre was immortalised in Charles Dickens's novel, 'Nicholas Nickleby', in which the eponymous hero and his companion, Smike, join Mr Vincent Crummles's theatrical company and perform there.

Portsmouth hosted a remarkable gathering of European leaders between 22 and 24 June 1814. This was the Visit of the Allied Sovereigns, to mark and celebrate what all believed was the end of hostilities against France. The Prince Regent presided over a gathering which included the King of Prussia, the Emperor of Russia, the Duke of Wellington and Marshal Blucher. The guests, their retinues and the people of Portsmouth gave themselves up to three days of glorious celebrations.

During the visit of the Allied Sovereigns in 1814, Marshal Blucher actually put up at the Crown Inn in the High Street with his accompanying staff.

It is not generally known that when Lord Nelson breakfasted at the George Hotel, on the morning of 14 September 1805, the crowds outside in the High Street were so great that he had to slip out through the back of the building into Penny Street. He made his way on foot down to the beach and, with Captain Hardy, threaded his way past the bathing machines and down to his boat.

Quebec House in Bath Square, Old Portsmouth is an early bathing house, built in the mid 18th century when the benefits of bathing in seawater were gaining currency. The bathing house was built by popular subscription. Some of its ground floor rooms still have trapdoors, through which bathers descended to the shingle and the saltwater beneath. Today, Quebec House is a private residence.

The man responsible for developing the elegant villas and terraces of early Southsea, a local architect and entrepreneur, lived at Dovercourt, Kent Road, now Portsmouth High School Junior School.

Portsmouth's fortifications were not demolished until the 1870s. The land released was used for a public park, Victoria Park, for playing fields for the naval and military personnel and for barracks. The City Museum and Records Office is housed in the one remaining block of the former Victoria and Clarence Barracks complex.

The railway line was built over the stretch of canal from Fratton Station to Portsmouth and Southsea Station. Goldsmith Avenue follows the route of the waterway from Milton to Fratton.

GOSPORT, FROM PORTSMOUTH c1965 G37109

SOUTHSEA, THE MINIATURE RAILWAY c1955 S161060

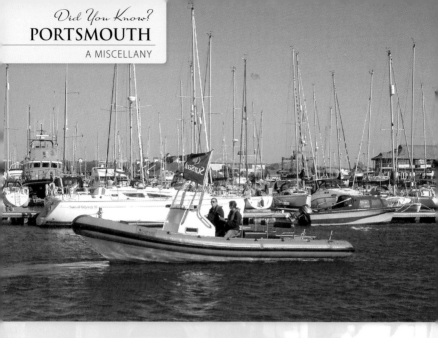

PORTSMOUTH, PORT SOLENT 2005 PI00708k

There have been four purpose-built town halls in Portsmouth: the 16th century building in the centre of the High Street opposite the Dolphin; its early 18th-century replacement; the early 19th century town hall next door to the Dolphin; and today's Guildhall, opened in 1890 and rebuilt after the Second World War, opening again in 1958. The Civic Offices were opened in 1974.

The Blue Posts Hotel in Broad Street was so-called because of the brightly-painted blue posts which flanked the entrance to the bar areas and the yard at the back of the building.

Portsmouth Cathedral was extended twice in the course of the 20th century. Work began before the Second World War to enlarge the building to a size commensurate with its status as the cathedral church of the new Anglican diocese of Portsmouth. The outbreak of war in 1939 put a stop to the work and a single-skin red brick wall was hastily put up at the west end of the half-completed nave. The project was completed finally in the 1980s in the spirit of the original intentions of Sir Charles Nicholson.

SOUTHSEA, A HOVERCRAFT ON THE SEAFRONT 2005 S161704k

Portsmouth possesses one of the finest collections of civic plate in the country. It includes several pieces acquired in the 16th century as well as a priceless collection of early 17th-century silver and silver-gilt standing cups.

There were fourteen breweries in Portsmouth in 1902. By the end of the century there were none.

The Guildhall was reduced to a smoking ruin by enemy air raids on the night of 10-11 January 1941, but the city's historic records and the priceless collection of civic plate survived the disaster in the basement of the Guildhall, being in a strongroom built by the security firm Chubb, who were themselves founded in Portsmouth in the 18th century.

The Guildhall might have survived the blitz of 10-11 January 1941 but for the fact that the water mains were also shattered that night and there was no water to put out the fires once they had gained a hold.

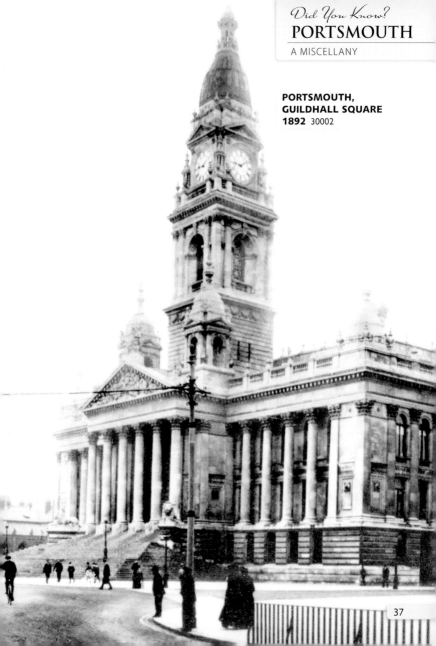

**PORTSMOUTH,
GUILDHALL SQUARE
1892** 30002

SOUTHSEA, THE 'D' DAY MEMORIAL c1955 S161059

1940

FRANCE AND THE LOW
COUNTRIES HAVING BEEN
OVERRUN WE LABOURED
ALONE TO OBSTRUCT
OUR COASTS WITH SUCH
BLOCKS AS THIS AGAINST
INVASION BY THE
ENEMIES OF FREEDOM

By 1939, the population of Portsmouth had risen to just over 250,000 people and the city's boundaries had reached their furthest extent, now embracing the mainland areas of Cosham, Paulsgrove and Wymering, Drayton and parts of Portchester.

During the Second World War, General Eisenhower's headquarters were at Southwick House, just outside Portsmouth, and it was there that he gave the historic 'order to go', which launched one of the greatest invasion offensives ever, to recapture Western Europe from Hitler's Germany - D-Day.

Portmouth was the centre of the 'D-Day 50' Commemorations in 1994 and, as in 1814, the city was the venue for a remarkable assembly of heads of the allied states, including the Presidents of the United States and of France. HM the Queen held a glittering banquet for her guests in the Guildhall and a Drumhead Service was held on Southsea Common the following day.

Portsmouth had a considerable corset industry in the 19th and early 20th centuries. There was a plentiful female labour force, many of whose menfolk were away at sea, so it was possible to keep wages low. Corsets were worn by men and women and several thousand women were employed in the trade, working either in their own homes or in local factories in the 19th century.

PORTSMOUTH, MILTON 2005 P100723k

The Gunwharf was Portsmouth's arsenal. Here the ordnance was kept, not only for ships, but also for the defences in general. There had been, from the 16th century, a gunwharf where ships unloaded their guns before they went into dock and picked them up on their way back to sea again.

Portsmouth is the largest fruit-importing port in the country.

SOUTHSEA, THE ROCK GARDENS c1955 S161023

**PORTSMOUTH HARBOUR AND
HMS 'VICTORY' 1890** 22754

43

SPORTING PORTSMOUTH

The Olympic athlete Roger Black was born in Portsmouth in 1966, and attended Portsmouth Grammar School where he was head boy. Amongst his impressive medal collection are a silver medal for the 400m from the 1996 Olympics in Atlanta, USA and another silver medal from the 1997 World Championships for the 4 x 400m relay.

Portsmouth-born Katy Sexton MBE became the first British female swimmer to win an individual gold medal at the 2003 World Championships in Barcelona in the 200m backstroke event. Katy is a member of Portsmouth Northsea Swimming Club.

Portsmouth Football Club has won the FA Cup twice in its history. In 1939 The Blues beat Wolves 4-1 to win the trophy, and in the 2007/8 season they beat Cardiff City 1-0. This win earned them a place in the 2008-09 UEFA Cup, the first time that the club has been involved in European football.

After Portsmouth FC won the FA Cup in 1939 fixtures were suspended because of the Second World War, and the trophy was stowed away in the strongroom in the basement of the Guildhall until the cessation of hostilities in 1945. For this reason, Portsmouth can claim to have held the FA Cup longer than any football club!

The colour of Portsmouth Football Club's original kit was salmon pink! It changed to white shirts and black shorts and socks in 1909, and in 1911 to the familiar royal blue shirts and white shorts.

One of the favourite chants sung by Portsmouth FC supporters around Fratton Park is the Pompey Chimes ('Play up Pompey, Pompey play up'). This originated with the Royal Artillery, a football team who played many of their home games at the United Services ground in Burnaby Road in the 1890s. Referees at these matches used the sound of the striking of the Guildhall clock to mark the end of the match at 4pm. The crowd would chant in time with the clock as it chimed the hour to encourage the referee to blow the final whistle. After the Royal Artillery were expelled from the FA Amateur Cup in the 1898-99 season many of their supporters turned to Portsmouth FC instead, bringing their Chimes chant with them.

The rivalry between Southampton and Portsmouth Football Clubs is well-known, but in former years there was equal rivalry between Portsmouth and Plymouth Argyle, referred to variously as the Naval Derby, the Dockyard Derby or the Battle of the Ports.

SOUTHSEA, THE ANCHOR OF HMS 'VICTORY' c1955 S161042

QUIZ QUESTIONS

Answers on page 50.

1. Which comic opera by Gilbert & Sullivan is set in Portsmouth Harbour?

2. Who built Portchester Castle in the late 3rd century, and why?

3. What is the device on Portsmouth's common seal?

4. Which royal wedding took place in the Governor's residence, the old Domus Dei, in Portsmouth in 1662?

5. In the second half of the 19th century, the Prime Minister Lord Palmerston was responsible for building a string of forts along the top of Portsdown to protect Portsmouth against a perceived threat from France. What are they called, and why?

6. Which historic sea voyage left Portsmouth in 1787?

7. Which famous person was born at 393 Commercial Road in Portsmouth in 1847?

8. What historic event for Portsmouth occurred in 1926?

9. What is the city motto of Portsmouth?

10. The novel 'A Study in Scarlet' was written in 1886 whilst the author lived in Portsmouth, working as a GP. It was the first novel in a series featuring which famous fictional detective?

SOUTHSEA, THE ENTRANCE TO THE CASTLE 2005 S161702k

47

RECIPE

BROCCOLI AND LEEK TART

Market gardening has been important in the southern part of Hampshire for many years, and in the 19th century vast quantities of cabbages and other vegetables were brought to the Portsmouth markets to supply the dockyards and hospitals. It was said at this time that Portsea Island produced the best broccoli in the kingdom!

Ingredients:

175g/6oz plain flour, sifted
115g/4oz butter or margarine
25g/1oz finely grated tasty cheese of choice
2 small leeks, sliced
75g/3oz small broccoli florets
150ml/ ¼ pint milk

2 beaten eggs
30ml/2 tablespoonfuls double cream
Ground mace to taste
Salt and black pepper
15g/ ½ oz flaked almonds, toasted, to garnish

Blend the flour, butter and cheese together either in a food processor or by hand until the mixture resembles fine breadcrumbs. Add salt to taste. Stir in 4-6 tablespoonfuls of cold water, mix and knead to form into a ball of pastry, then chill the pastry in the fridge for about 15 minutes.

Preheat the oven to 190°C/375°F/Gas Mark 5. Roll out the pastry on a floured surface and use it to line a 20cm/8inch flan dish or tin. Line the pastry case with greaseproof paper and fill with baking beans. Bake the pastry case blind for 15 minutes, then remove the beans and paper and cook for a further 5 minutes to dry out the base.

Place the milk in a saucepan and bring to the boil, then add the vegetables, reduce the heat and simmer gently for 2-3 minutes. Strain the milk into a bowl and whisk in the eggs, mace, seasoning and cream. Arrange the vegetables in the pastry case and pour the egg mixture over them. Bake for 20 minutes, or until the filling is just firm to the touch. Sprinkle with the toasted almonds before serving.

Can be eaten hot or cold.

RECIPE

NELSON SQUARES

This recipe is a reference to Admiral Lord Nelson, whose flagship 'Victory' is a major visitor attraction in Portsmouth. The mixed peel may be replaced by an extra 50g/2oz of dried fruit, if preferred.

Ingredients:

225g/8oz stale white bread, with crusts removed

300ml/ ½ pint milk

115g/4oz currants or raisins, or a mixture of both

50g/2oz mixed peel, finely chopped

50g/2oz suet

50g/2oz demerara sugar

1-2 level teaspoonfuls mixed spice, to taste

1 egg for the mixture

500g/1lb shortcrust pastry or puff-pastry, whichever is preferred (readymade is fine)

1 beaten egg or a little extra milk for sealing and glazing the pastry

Soak the bread in the milk for about half an hour, then beat out any lumps to leave a smooth mixture. Add the dried fruit, mixed peel, suet, sugar and mixed spice and mix well. Mix in the egg, and add a little extra milk if the mixture is too stiff to spread easily.

Pre-heat the oven to 180°C/350°F/Gas Mark 4.

Grease a deep 22cm/9 inch-square baking tin. Roll out the pastry and cut into two sections, making one approx 28cm/11 inches square, and the other approx 22cm/9 inches square. Use the bigger section to line the base of the baking tin - there should be enough for the pastry to come up the sides of the tin. Spread the fruit mixture evenly over the pastry in the tin, leaving a slight gap around the sides. Brush the edge of the pastry with some of the beaten egg or milk, cover the mixture with the other square of pastry and pinch the edges together with the bottom layer to seal them together and enclose the mixture.

Brush the surface of the pastry with milk or beaten egg and prick some holes in the surface with a fork. Bake in the oven for 1½ to 2 hours, until the pastry is golden brown. Leave to cool in the tin then turn out, sprinkle with sugar and cut into squares before serving.

QUIZ ANSWERS

1. 'H M S Pinafore'.

2. The Belgian seaman, and later the rebel Roman emperor, Marcus Aurelius Carausius, to help protect Roman Britain from North Sea pirates. The great walled fortress at the top of Portsmouth Harbour was part of a defensive line of similar forts - the forts of the 'Saxon Shore' - stretching from the Wash to the Solent.

3. A ship with castle and furled sail, with a crescent on the left of the mast and a star on the right.

4. The marriage of King Charles II and the Portuguese princess, Catherine of Braganza. The marriage could not take place in Portsmouth's parish church of St Thomas because that building had been badly damaged by Parliamentarian guns during the Civil War. A wedding gift of a silver and crystal salt-cellar was given to the newly-married couple by the people of Portsmouth. The diarist Samuel Pepys was greatly impressed with the gift, describing it as 'a salt-sellar of silver, the walls of cristall, with four Eagles and four greyhounds standing up at top to bear up a dish - which endeed is one of the neatest pieces of plate that ever I saw.'

5. The real names of the forts are Wallington, Nelson, Southwick, Widley, Purbrook and Farlington, but they were often referred to as 'Palmerston's Follies'. The forts were deliberately built to face north in order to repudiate an enemy force which might have landed further along the coast and attempted to surprise

the town from the north. The project took over 20 years to complete, by which time the threat from France had disappeared. There was a great deal of opposition to the whole project in parliament when it was first planned as many members felt that Lord Palmerston was reacting to an exaggerated threat, but in the course of one angry exchange between the Prime Minister and his Chancellor of the Exchequer, Mr Gladstone, who was threatening to resign, Lord Palmerston declared that it would be better to lose Gladstone than lose Portsmouth.

6. The 'First Fleet' of HMS 'Sirius', the brig 'Supply' and nine transports carrying convicts, which set sail from Spithead for New South Wales on 13th May 1787 to establish the first Australian penal colony.

7. The writer Charles Dickens. His father, John Dickens, was a clerk in the Navy Pay Office.

8. In 1926 Portsmouth was declared a city.

9. The city's motto is 'Heaven's Light Our Guide'. It was the motto of the Order of the Star of India. The star of the order has wavy rays of gold issuing from the centre in the style of the star on the arms of Portsmouth - an Islamic device. 'Heaven's Light Our Guide' was also the motto of the old Indian troopships, which embarked their passengers at Portsmouth.

10. Sherlock Holmes. The author, Arthur Conan Doyle, lived and worked at No 1 Bush Villas, Elm Grove in Southsea. The building was destroyed during the air-raids of the Second World War.

SOUTHSEA, THE CANOE LAKE c1955   S161049

FRANCIS FRITH

PIONEER VICTORIAN PHOTOGRAPHER

Francis Frith, founder of the world-famous photographic archive, was a complex and multi-talented man. A devout Quaker and a highly successful Victorian businessman, he was philosophical by nature and pioneering in outlook. By 1855 he had already established a wholesale grocery business in Liverpool, and sold it for the astonishing sum of £200,000, which is the equivalent today of over £15,000,000. Now in his thirties, and captivated by the new science of photography, Frith set out on a series of pioneering journeys up the Nile and to the Near East.

INTRIGUE AND EXPLORATION

He was the first photographer to venture beyond the sixth cataract of the Nile. Africa was still the mysterious 'Dark Continent', and Stanley and Livingstone's historic meeting was a decade into the future. The conditions for picture taking confound belief. He laboured for hours in his wicker dark-room in the sweltering heat of the desert, while the volatile chemicals fizzed dangerously in their trays. Back in London he exhibited his photographs and was 'rapturously cheered' by members of the Royal Society. His reputation as a photographer was made overnight.

VENTURE OF A LIFE-TIME

By the 1870s the railways had threaded their way across the country, and Bank Holidays and half-day Saturdays had been made obligatory by Act of Parliament. All of a sudden the working man and his family were able to enjoy days out, take holidays, and see a little more of the world.

With typical business acumen, Francis Frith foresaw that these new tourists would enjoy having souvenirs to commemorate their days out. For the next thirty years he travelled the country by train and by pony and trap, producing fine photographs of seaside resorts and beauty spots that were keenly bought by millions of Victorians. These prints were painstakingly pasted into family albums and pored over during the dark nights of winter, rekindling precious memories of summer excursions. Frith's studio was soon supplying retail shops all over the country, and by 1890 F Frith & Co had become the greatest specialist photographic publishing company in the world, with over 2,000 sales outlets, and pioneered the picture postcard.

FRANCIS FRITH'S LEGACY

Francis Frith had died in 1898 at his villa in Cannes, his great project still growing. By 1970 the archive he created contained over a third of a million pictures showing 7,000 British towns and villages.

Frith's legacy to us today is of immense significance and value, for the magnificent archive of evocative photographs he created provides a unique record of change in the cities, towns and villages throughout Britain over a century and more. Frith and his fellow studio photographers revisited locations many times down the years to update their views, compiling for us an enthralling and colourful pageant of British life and character.

We are fortunate that Frith was dedicated to recording the minutiae of everyday life. For it is this sheer wealth of visual data, the painstaking chronicle of changes in dress, transport, street layouts, buildings, housing and landscape that captivates us so much today, offering us a powerful link with the past and with the lives of our ancestors.

Computers have now made it possible for Frith's many thousands of images to be accessed almost instantly. The archive offers every one of us an opportunity to examine the places where we and our families have lived and worked down the years. Its images, depicting our shared past, are now bringing pleasure and enlightenment to millions around the world a century and more after his death.

For further information visit: www.francisfrith.com

INTERIOR DECORATION

Frith's photographs can be seen framed and as giant wall murals in thousands of pubs, restaurants, hotels, banks, retail stores and other public buildings throughout Britain. These provide interesting and attractive décor, generating strong local interest and acting as a powerful reminder of gentler days in our increasingly busy and frenetic world.

FRITH PRODUCTS

All Frith photographs are available as prints and posters in a variety of different sizes and styles. In the UK we also offer a range of other gift and stationery products illustrated with Frith photographs, although many of these are not available for delivery outside the UK – see our web site for more information on the products available for delivery in your country.

THE INTERNET

Over 100,000 photographs of Britain can be viewed and purchased on the Frith web site. The web site also includes memories and reminiscences contributed by our customers, who have personal knowledge of localities and of the people and properties depicted in Frith photographs. If you wish to learn more about a specific town or village you may find these reminiscences fascinating to browse. Why not add your own comments if you think they would be of interest to others? See **www.francisfrith.com**

PLEASE HELP US BRING FRITH'S PHOTOGRAPHS TO LIFE

Our authors do their best to recount the history of the places they write about. They give insights into how particular towns and villages developed, they describe the architecture of streets and buildings, and they discuss the lives of famous people who lived there. But however knowledgeable our authors are, the story they tell is necessarily incomplete.

Frith's photographs are so much more than plain historical documents. They are living proofs of the flow of human life down the generations. They show real people at real moments in history; and each of those people is the son or daughter of someone, the brother or sister, aunt or uncle, grandfather or grandmother of someone else. All of them lived, worked and played in the streets depicted in Frith's photographs.

We would be grateful if you would give us your insights into the places shown in our photographs: the streets and buildings, the shops, businesses and industries. Post your memories of life in those streets on the Frith website: what it was like growing up there, who ran the local shop and what shopping was like years ago; if your workplace is shown tell us about your working day and what the building is used for now. Read other visitors' memories and reconnect with your shared local history and heritage. With your help more and more Frith photographs can be brought to life, and vital memories preserved for posterity, and for the benefit of historians in the future.

Wherever possible, we will try to include some of your comments in future editions of our books. Moreover, if you spot errors in dates, titles or other facts, please let us know, because our archive records are not always completely accurate—they rely on 140 years of human endeavour and hand-compiled records. You can email us using the contact form on the website.

Thank you!

For further information, trade, or author enquiries
please contact us at the address below:

**The Francis Frith Collection, Oakley Business Park,
Wylye Road, Dinton, Wiltshire SP3 5EU.**

Tel: +44 (0)1722 716 376 Fax: +44 (0)1722 716 881
e-mail: sales@francisfrith.co.uk **www.francisfrith.com**